O'REILLY®
Strata
Making Data Work

Learn how data into decisions.

From startups to the Fortune 500, smart companies are betting on data-driven insight, seizing the opportunities that are emerging from the convergence of four powerful trends:

- New methods of collecting, managing, and analyzing data

- Cloud computing that offers inexpensive storage and flexible, on-demand computing power for massive data sets

- Visualization techniques that turn complex data into images that tell a compelling story

- Tools that make the power of data available to anyone

Get control over big data and turn it into insight with O'Reilly's Strata offerings. Find the inspiration and information to create new products or revive existing ones, understand customer behavior, and get the data edge.

O'REILLY®

Visit oreilly.com/data to learn more.

©2011 O'Reilly Media, Inc. O'Reilly logo is a registered trademark of O'Reilly Media, Inc.

Big Data Glossary

Pete Warden

O'REILLY®

Beijing · Cambridge · Farnham · Köln · Sebastopol · Tokyo

Big Data Glossary
by Pete Warden

Copyright © 2011 Pete Warden. All rights reserved.
Printed in the United States of America.

Published by O'Reilly Media, Inc., 1005 Gravenstein Highway North, Sebastopol, CA 95472.

O'Reilly books may be purchased for educational, business, or sales promotional use. Online editions are also available for most titles (*http://my.safaribooksonline.com*). For more information, contact our corporate/institutional sales department: (800) 998-9938 or *corporate@oreilly.com*.

Editor: Mike Loukides
Production Editor: Teresa Elsey

Cover Designer: Karen Montgomery
Interior Designer: David Futato
Illustrator: Robert Romano

Nutshell Handbook, the Nutshell Handbook logo, and the O'Reilly logo are registered trademarks of O'Reilly Media, Inc. *Big Data Glossary*, the image of an elephant seal, and related trade dress are trademarks of O'Reilly Media, Inc.

Many of the designations used by manufacturers and sellers to distinguish their products are claimed as trademarks. Where those designations appear in this book, and O'Reilly Media, Inc., was aware of a trademark claim, the designations have been printed in caps or initial caps.

While every precaution has been taken in the preparation of this book, the publisher and authors assume no responsibility for errors or omissions, or for damages resulting from the use of the information contained herein.

ISBN: 978-1-449-31459-0

[LSI]

1315581672

Table of Contents

Preface

There's been a massive amount of innovation in data tools over the last few years, thanks to a few key trends:

Learning from the Web
> Techniques originally developed by website developers coping with scaling issues are increasingly being applied to other domains.

CS+?=$$$
> Google has proven that research techniques from computer science can be effective at solving problems and creating value in many real-world situations. That's led to increased interest in cross-pollination and investment in academic research from commercial organizations.

Cheap hardware
> Now that machines with a decent amount of processing power can be hired for just a few cents an hour, many more people can afford to do large-scale data processing. They can't afford the traditional high prices of professional data software, though, so they've turned to open source alternatives.

These trends have led to a Cambrian explosion of new tools, which means that when you're planning a new data project, you have a lot to choose from. This guide aims to help you make those choices by describing each tool from the perspective of a developer looking to use it in an application. Wherever possible, this will be from my firsthand experiences or from those of colleagues who have used the systems in production environments. I've made a deliberate choice to include my own opinions and impressions, so you should see this guide as a starting point for exploring the tools, not the final word. I'll do my best to explain what I like about each service, but your tastes and requirements may well be quite different.

Since the goal is to help experienced engineers navigate the new data landscape, this guide only covers tools that have been created or risen to prominence in the last few years. For example, Postgres is not covered because it's been widely used for over a decade, but its Greenplum derivative is newer and less well-known, so it is included.

Conventions Used in This Book

The following typographical conventions are used in this book:

Italic
> Indicates new terms, URLs, email addresses, filenames, and file extensions.

`Constant width`
> Used for program listings, as well as within paragraphs to refer to program elements such as variable or function names, databases, data types, environment variables, statements, and keywords.

`Constant width bold`
> Shows commands or other text that should be typed literally by the user.

`Constant width italic`
> Shows text that should be replaced with user-supplied values or by values determined by context.

> This icon signifies a tip, suggestion, or general note.

> This icon indicates a warning or caution.

Using Code Examples

This book is here to help you get your job done. In general, you may use the code in this book in your programs and documentation. You do not need to contact us for permission unless you're reproducing a significant portion of the code. For example, writing a program that uses several chunks of code from this book does not require permission. Selling or distributing a CD-ROM of examples from O'Reilly books does require permission. Answering a question by citing this book and quoting example code does not require permission. Incorporating a significant amount of example code from this book into your product's documentation does require permission.

We appreciate, but do not require, attribution. An attribution usually includes the title, author, publisher, and ISBN. For example: "*Big Data Glossary* by Pete Warden (O'Reilly). Copyright 2011 Pete Warden, 978-1-449-31459-0."

If you feel your use of code examples falls outside fair use or the permission given above, feel free to contact us at *permissions@oreilly.com*.

Safari® Books Online

Safari Books Online is an on-demand digital library that lets you easily search over 7,500 technology and creative reference books and videos to find the answers you need quickly.

With a subscription, you can read any page and watch any video from our library online. Read books on your cell phone and mobile devices. Access new titles before they are available for print, and get exclusive access to manuscripts in development and post feedback for the authors. Copy and paste code samples, organize your favorites, download chapters, bookmark key sections, create notes, print out pages, and benefit from tons of other time-saving features.

O'Reilly Media has uploaded this book to the Safari Books Online service. To have full digital access to this book and others on similar topics from O'Reilly and other publishers, sign up for free at *http://my.safaribooksonline.com*.

How to Contact Us

Please address comments and questions concerning this book to the publisher:

O'Reilly Media, Inc.
1005 Gravenstein Highway North
Sebastopol, CA 95472
800-998-9938 (in the United States or Canada)
707-829-0515 (international or local)
707-829-0104 (fax)

We have a web page for this book, where we list errata, examples, and any additional information. You can access this page at:

http://www.oreilly.com/catalog/9781449314590

To comment or ask technical questions about this book, send email to:

bookquestions@oreilly.com

For more information about our books, courses, conferences, and news, see our website at *http://www.oreilly.com*.

Find us on Facebook: *http://facebook.com/oreilly*

Follow us on Twitter: *http://twitter.com/oreillymedia*

Watch us on YouTube: *http://www.youtube.com/oreillymedia*

CHAPTER 1

Terms

These new tools need some shorthand labels to describe their properties, and since they're likely to be unfamiliar to traditional database users, I'll start off with a few definitions.

Document-Oriented

In a traditional relational database, the user begins by specifying a series of column types and names for a table. Information is then added as rows of values, with each of those named columns as a cell of each row. You can't have additional values that weren't specified when you created the table, and every value must be present, even if it's as a NULL value.

Document stores instead let you enter each record as a series of names with associated values, which you can picture being like a JavaScript object, a Python dictionary, or a Ruby hash. You don't specify ahead of time what names will be in each table using a schema. In theory, each record could contain a completely different set of named values, though in practice, the application layer often relies on an informal schema, with the client code expecting certain named values to be present.

The key advantage of this document-oriented approach is its flexibility. You can add or remove the equivalent of columns with no penalty, as long as the application layer doesn't rely on the values that were removed. A good analogy is the difference between languages where you declare the types of variables ahead of time, and those where the type is inferred by the compiler or interpreter. You lose information that can be used to automatically check correctness and optimize for performance, but it becomes a lot easier to prototype and experiment.

Key/Value Stores

The memcached (*http://memcached.org/*) system introduced a lot of web programmers to the power of treating a data store like a giant associative array, reading and writing values based purely on a unique key. It leads to a very simple interface, with three primitive operations to get the data associated with a particular key, to store some data against a key, and to delete a key and its data. Unlike relational databases, with a pure key/value store, it's impossible to run queries, though some may offer extensions, like the ability to find all the keys that match a wild-carded expression. This means that the application code has to handle building any complex operations out of the primitive calls it can make to the store.

Why would any developer want to do that extra work? With more complex databases, you're often paying a penalty in complexity or performance for features you may not care about, like full ACID (*http://en.wikipedia.org/wiki/ACID*) compliance. With key/value stores, you're given very basic building blocks that have very predictable performance characteristics, and you can create the more complex operations using the same language as the rest of your application.

A lot of the databases listed here try to retain the simplicity of a pure key/value store interface, but with some extra features added to meet common requirements. It seems likely that there's a sweet spot of functionality that retains some of the advantages of minimal key/value stores without requiring quite as much duplicated effort from the application developer.

Horizontal or Vertical Scaling

Traditional database architectures are designed to run well on a single machine, and the simplest way to handle larger volumes of operations is to upgrade the machine with a faster processor or more memory. That approach to increasing speed is known as vertical scaling. More recent data processing systems, such as Hadoop and Cassandra, are designed to run on clusters of comparatively low-specification servers, and so the easiest way to handle more data is to add more of those machines to the cluster. This horizontal scaling approach tends to be cheaper as the number of operations and the size of the data increases, and the very largest data processing pipelines are all built on a horizontal model. There is a cost to this approach, though. Writing distributed data handling code is tricky and involves tradeoffs between speed, scalability, fault tolerance, and traditional database goals like atomicity and consistency.

MapReduce

MapReduce is an algorithm design pattern that originated in the functional programming world. It consists of three steps. First, you write a mapper function or script that goes through your input data and outputs a series of keys and values to use in calculating the results. The keys are used to cluster together bits of data that will be needed to calculate a single output result. The unordered list of keys and values is then put through a sort step that ensures that all the fragments that have the same key are next to one another in the file. The reducer stage then goes through the sorted output and receives all of the values that have the same key in a contiguous block.

That may sound like a very roundabout way of building your algorithms, but its prime virtue is that it removes unplanned random accesses, with all scattering and gathering handled in the sorting phase. Even on single machines, this boosts performance, thanks to the increased locality of memory accesses, but it also allows the process to be split across a large number of machines easily, by dealing with the input in many independent chunks and partitioning the data based on the key.

Hadoop is the best-known public system for running MapReduce algorithms, but many modern databases, such as MongoDB, also support it as an option. It's worthwhile even in a fairly traditional system, since if you can write your query in a MapReduce form, you'll be able to run it efficiently on as many machines as you have available.

Sharding

Any database that's spread across multiple machines needs some scheme to decide which machines a given piece of data should be stored on. A sharding system makes this decision for each row in a table, using its key. In the simplest case, the application programmer will specify an explicit rule to use for sharding. For example, if you had a ten machine cluster and a numerical key, you might use the last decimal digit of the key to decide which machine to store data on. Since both the storing and retrieval code knows about this rule, when you need to get the row it's possible to go directly to the machine that holds it.

The biggest problems with sharding are splitting the data evenly across machines and dealing with changes in the size of the cluster. Using the same example, imagine that the numerical keys often end in zero; that will lead to an extremely unbalanced distribution where a single machine is overused and becomes a bottleneck. If the cluster size is expanded from ten to fifteen machines, we could switch to a modulo fifteen scheme for assigning data, but it would require a wholesale shuffling of all the data on the cluster.

To ease the pain of these problems, more complex schemes are used to split up the data. Some of these rely on a central directory that holds the locations of particular keys. This level of indirection allows data to be moved between machines when a particular shard grows too large (to rebalance the distribution), at the cost of requiring an extra lookup in the directory for each operation. The directory's information is usually fairly small and reasonably static, though, so it's a good candidate for local caching, as long as the infrequent changes are spotted.

Another popular approach is the use of consistent hashing (*http://michaelnielsen.org/blog/consistent-hashing/*) for the sharding. This technique uses a small table splitting the possible range of hash values into ranges, with one assigned to each shard. The lookup data needed by clients is extremely lightweight, with just a couple of numerical values per node, so it can be shared and cached efficiently, but it has enough flexibility to allow fast rebalancing of the value distributions when nodes are added and removed, or even just when one node becomes overloaded, unlike fixed modulo functions.

CHAPTER 2

NoSQL Databases

A few years ago, web programmers started to use the memcached (*http://memcached .org/*) system to temporarily store data in RAM, so frequently used values could be retrieved very quickly, rather than relying on a slower path accessing the full database from disk. This coding pattern required all of the data accesses to be written using only key/value primitives, initially in addition to the traditional SQL queries on the main database. As developers got more comfortable with the approach, they started to experiment with databases that used a key/value interface for the persistent storage as well as the cache, since they already had to express most of their queries in that form anyway. This is a rare example of the removal of an abstraction layer, since the key/value interface is less expressive and lower-level than a query language like SQL. These systems do require more work from an application developer, but they also offer a lot more flexibility and control over the work the database is performing. The cut-down interface also makes it easier for database developers to create new and experimental systems to try out new solutions to tough requirements like very large-scale, widely distributed data sets or high throughput applications.

This widespread demand for solutions, and the comparative ease of developing new systems, has led to a flowering of new databases. The main thing they have in common is that none of them support the traditional SQL interface, which has led to the movement being dubbed NoSQL. It's a bit misleading, though, since almost every production environment that they're used in also has an SQL-based database for anything that requires flexible queries and reliable transactions, and as the products mature, it's likely that some of them will start supporting the language as an option. If "NoSQL" seems too combative, think of it as "NotOnlySQL." These are all tools designed to trade the reliability and ease-of-use of traditional databases for the flexibility and performance required by new problems developers are encountering.

With so many different systems appearing, such a variety of design tradeoffs, and such a short track record for most, this list is inevitably incomplete and somewhat subjective. I'll be providing a summary of my own experiences with and impressions of each database, but I encourage you to check out their official web pages to get the most up-to-date and complete view.

MongoDB (*http://www.mongodb.org*)

Mongo, whose name comes from "humongous" (*http://www.snailinaturtleneck.com/blog/2010/08/23/history-of-mongodb/*), is a database aimed at developers with fairly large data sets, but who want something that's low maintenance and easy to work with. It's a document-oriented system, with records that look similar to JSON objects with the ability to store and query on nested attributes. From my own experience, a big advantage is the proactive support from the developers employed by 10gen (*http://www.10gen.com/*), the commercial company that originated and supports the open source project. I've always had quick and helpful responses both on the IRC channel (*irc://irc.freenode.net/#mongodb*) and mailing list (*http://groups.google.com/group/mongodb-user*), something that's crucial when you're dealing with comparatively young technologies like these.

It supports automatic sharding (*http://www.mongodb.org/display/DOCS/Sharding*) and MapReduce operations (*http://www.mongodb.org/display/DOCS/MapReduce*). Queries are written in JavaScript, with an interactive shell available, and bindings for all of the other popular languages.

```
Spike:~ petewarden$ mongo
MongoDB shell version: 1.0.1
url: test
connecting to: test
type "help" for help
> db.users.save({name:"Pete Warden", eyes:"Blue"});
> db.users.find({name:"Pete Warden"});
{"_id" : ObjectId( "4e48683fc6092f1f77ffac16")  , "name" : "Pete Warden" , "eyes" : "Blue"}
>
```

- Quickstart documentation (*http://www.mongodb.org/display/DOCS/Quickstart*)

CouchDB (*http://couchdb.apache.org*)

CouchDB is similar in many ways to MongoDB, as a document-oriented database with a JavaScript interface, but it differs in how it supports querying, scaling, and versioning. It uses a multiversion concurrency control approach, which helps with problems that require access to the state of data at various times, but it does involve more work on the client side to handle clashes on writes, and periodic garbage collection cycles have to be run to remove old data. It doesn't have a good built-in method for horizontal scalability, but there are various external solutions like BigCouch (*https://github.com/cloudant/bigcouch*), Lounge (*http://tilgovi.github.com/couchdb-lounge/*), and Pillow (*https://github.com/khellan/Pillow*) to handle splitting data and processing across a cluster of machines.

You query the data by writing JavaScript MapReduce functions called views, an approach that makes it easy for the system to do the processing in a distributed way. Views offer a lot of power and flexibility, but they can be a bit overwhelming for simple queries.

- Getting started with CouchDB (*http://net.tutsplus.com/tutorials/getting-started -with-couchdb/*)

Cassandra (*http://cassandra.apache.org*)

Originally an internal Facebook project, Cassandra was open sourced a few years ago and has become the standard distributed database for situations where it's worth investing the time to learn a complex system in return for a lot of power and flexibility. Traditionally, it was a long struggle just to set up a working cluster, but as the project matures, that has become a lot easier.

It's a distributed key/value system, with highly structured values that are held in a hierarchy similar to the classic database/table levels, with the equivalents being keyspaces and column families. It's very close to the data model used by Google's BigTable, which you can find described in "BigTable" on page 8. By default, the data is sharded and balanced automatically using consistent hashing on key ranges, though other schemes can be configured. The data structures are optimized for consistent write performance, at the cost of occasionally slow read operations. One very useful feature is the ability to specify how many nodes must agree before a read or write operation completes. Setting the *consistency level* allows you to tune the CAP (*http://www.julian browne.com/article/viewer/brewers-cap-theorem*) tradeoffs for your particular application, to prioritize speed over consistency or vice versa.

The lowest-level interface to Cassandra is through Thrift (*http://thrift.apache.org/*), but there are friendlier clients available for most major languages (*http://wiki.apache.org/ cassandra/ClientOptions*). The recommended option for running queries is through Hadoop (*http://wiki.apache.org/cassandra/HadoopSupport*). You can install Hadoop directly on the same cluster to ensure locality of access, and there's also a distribution of Hadoop integrated with Cassandra (*http://www.datastax.com/brisk*) available from DataStax (*http://www.datastax.com/*).

There is a command-line interface that lets you perform basic administration tasks, but it's quite bare bones. It is recommended that you choose initial tokens (*http://petewar den.typepad.com/searchbrowser/2011/07/cassandra-initial-tokens-table.html*) when you first set up your cluster, but otherwise the decentralized architecture is fairly low-maintenance, barring major problems.

- Up and running with Cassandra (*http://blog.evanweaver.com/2009/07/06/up-and -running-with-cassandra/*)

Redis (*http://redis.io*)

Two features make Redis stand out: it keeps the entire database in RAM, and its values can be complex data structures. Though the entire dataset is kept in memory, it's also backed up on disk periodically, so you can use it as a persistent database. This approach does offer fast and predictable performance, but speed falls off a cliff if the size of your data expands beyond available memory and the operating system starts paging virtual memory to handle accesses. This won't be a problem if you have small or predictably sized storage needs, but it does require a bit of forward planning as you're developing applications. You can deal with larger data sets by clustering multiple machines together, but the sharding is currently handled (*http://antirez.com/post/redis-presharding.html*) at the client level (*http://blog.zawodny.com/2011/02/26/redis-sharding-at-craigslist/*). There is an experimental branch (*http://antirez.com/post/2-4-and-other-news.html*) of the code under active development that supports clustering at the server level.

The support for complex data structures is impressive, with a large number of list and set operations handled quickly on the server side. It makes it easy to do things like appending to the end of a value that's a list, and then trim the list so that it only holds the most recent 100 items. These capabilities do make it easier to limit the growth of your data than it would be in most systems, as well as making life easier for application developers.

- Interactive tutorial (*http://try.redis-db.com/*)

BigTable (*http://labs.google.com/papers/bigtable.html*)

BigTable is only available to developers outside Google as the foundation of the App Engine datastore (*http://code.google.com/appengine/docs/python/datastore/overview.html*). Despite that, as one of the pioneering alternative databases, it's worth looking at.

It has a more complex structure and interface than many NoSQL datastores, with a hierarchy and multidimensional access. The first level, much like traditional relational databases, is a table holding data. Each table is split into multiple rows, with each row addressed with a unique key string. The values inside the row are arranged into cells, with each cell identified by a column family identifier, a column name, and a timestamp, each of which I'll explain below.

The row keys are stored in ascending order within file chunks called shards. This ensures that operations accessing continuous ranges of keys are efficient, though it does mean you have to think about the likely order you'll be reading your keys in. In one example, Google reversed the domain names of URLs they were using as keys so that all links from similar domains were nearby; for example, *com.google.maps/index.html* was near *com.google.www/index.html*.

You can think of a column family as something like a type or a class in a programming language. Each represents a set of data values that all have some common properties; for example, one might hold the HTML content of web pages, while another might be designed to contain a language identifier string. There's only expected to be a small number of these families per table, and they should be altered infrequently, so in practice they're often chosen when the table is created. They can have properties, constraints, and behaviors associated with them.

Column names are confusingly not much like column names in a relational database. They are defined dynamically, rather than specified ahead of time, and they often hold actual data themselves. If a column family represented inbound links to a page, the column name might be the URL of the page that the link is from, with the cell contents holding the link's text. The timestamp allows a given cell to have multiple versions over time, as well as making it possible to expire or garbage collect old data.

A given piece of data can be uniquely addressed by looking in a table for the full identifier that conceptually looks like row key, then column family, then column name, and finally timestamp. You can easily read all the values for a given row key in a particular column family, so you could actually think of the column family as being the closest comparison to a column in a relational database.

As you might expect from Google, BigTable is designed to handle very large data loads by running on big clusters of commodity hardware. It has per-row transaction guarantees, but it doesn't offer any way to atomically alter larger numbers of rows. It uses the Google File System as its underlying storage, which keeps redundant copies of all the persistent files so that failures can be recovered from.

HBase (*http://hbase.apache.org*)

HBase was designed as an open source clone of Google's BigTable, so unsurprisingly it has a very similar interface, and it relies on a clone of the Google File System called HDFS (*http://hadoop.apache.org/hdfs/*). It supports the same data structure of tables, row keys, column families, column names, timestamps, and cell values, though it is recommended that each table have no more than two or three families for performance reasons.

HBase is well integrated with the main Hadoop project (*http://hadoop.apache.org/*), so it's easy to write and read to the database from a MapReduce job running on the system. One thing to watch out for is that the latency on individual reads and writes can be comparatively slow, since it's a distributed system and the operations will involve some network traffic. HBase is at its best when it's accessed in a distributed fashion by many clients. If you're doing serialized reads and writes you may need to think about a caching strategy.

- Understanding HBase (*http://jimbojw.com/wiki/index.php?title=Understanding _Hbase_and_BigTable*)

Hypertable (*http://www.hypertable.org*)

Hypertable is another open source clone of BigTable. It's written in C++, rather than Java like HBase, and has focused its energies on high performance. Otherwise, its interface follows in BigTable's footsteps, with the same column family and timestamping concepts.

Voldemort (*http://project-voldemort.com*)

An open source clone of Amazon's Dynamo database (*http://s3.amazonaws.com/AllTh ingsDistributed/sosp/amazon-dynamo-sosp2007.pdf*) created by LinkedIn, Voldemort has a classic three-operation key/value interface, but with a sophisticated backend architecture to handle running on large distributed clusters. It uses consistent hashing to allow fast lookups of the storage locations for particular keys, and it has versioning control to handle inconsistent values. A read operation may actually return multiple values for a given key if they were written by different clients at nearly the same time. This then puts the burden on the application to take some sensible recovery actions when it gets multiple values, based on its knowledge of the meaning of the data being written. The example that Amazon uses is a shopping cart, where the set of items could be unioned together, losing any deliberate deletions but retaining any added items, which obviously makes sense—from a revenue perspective, at least!

Riak (*http://wiki.basho.com*)

Like Voldemort, Riak was inspired by Amazon's Dynamo database, and it offers a key/value interface and is designed to run on large distributed clusters. It also uses consistent hashing and a gossip protocol to avoid the need for the kind of centralized index server that BigTable requires, along with versioning to handle update conflicts. Querying is handled using MapReduce functions written in either Erlang or JavaScript. It's open source under an Apache license, but there's also a closed source commercial version with some special features designed for enterprise customers.

ZooKeeper (*http://zookeeper.apache.org*)

When you're running a service distributed across a large cluster of machines, even tasks like reading configuration information, which are simple on single-machine systems, can be hard to implement reliably. The ZooKeeper framework was originally built at Yahoo! to make it easy for the company's applications to access configuration information in a robust and easy-to-understand way, but it has since grown to offer a lot of features that help coordinate work across distributed clusters. One way to think of it is as a very specialized key/value store, with an interface that looks a lot like a filesystem and supports operations like watching callbacks, write consensus, and transaction IDs that are often needed for coordinating distributed algorithms.

This has allowed it to act as a foundation layer for services like LinkedIn's Norbert (*https://github.com/rhavyn/norbert*), a flexible framework for managing clusters of machines. ZooKeeper itself is built to run in a distributed way across a number of machines, and it's designed to offer very fast reads, at the expense of writes that get slower the more servers are used to host the service.

- Implementing primitives with ZooKeeper (*https://cwiki.apache.org/confluence/display/ZOOKEEPER/Tutorial*)

CHAPTER 3

MapReduce

In the traditional relational database world, all processing happens after the information has been loaded into the store, using a specialized query language on highly structured and optimized data structures. The approach pioneered by Google, and adopted by many other web companies, is to instead create a pipeline that reads and writes to arbitrary file formats, with intermediate results being passed between stages as files, with the computation spread across many machines. Typically based around the MapReduce approach to distributing work, this approach requires a whole new set of tools, which I'll describe below.

Hadoop (*http://hadoop.apache.org*)

Originally developed by Yahoo! as a clone of Google's MapReduce infrastructure, but subsequently open sourced, Hadoop takes care of running your code across a cluster of machines. Its responsibilities include chunking up the input data, sending it to each machine, running your code on each chunk, checking that the code ran, passing any results either on to further processing stages or to the final output location, performing the sort that occurs between the map and reduce stages and sending each chunk of that sorted data to the right machine, and writing debugging information on each job's progress, among other things.

As you might guess from that list of requirements, it's quite a complex system, but thankfully it has been battle-tested by a lot of users. There's a lot going on under the hood, but most of the time, as a developer, you only have to supply the code and data, and it just works. Its popularity also means that there's a large ecosystem of related tools, some that making writing individual processing steps easier, and others that orchestrate more complex jobs that require many inputs and steps. As a novice user, the best place to get started is by learning to write a *streaming job* in your favorite scripting language, since that lets you ignore the gory details of what's going on behind the scenes.

As a mature project, one of Hadoop's biggest strengths is the collection of debugging and reporting tools it has built in. Most of these are accessible through a web interface that holds details of all running and completed jobs and lets you drill down to the error and warning log files.

Quick Links

master Hadoop Map/Reduce Administration

State: RUNNING
Started: Sat Aug 13 03:35:53 UTC 2011
Version: 0.20.203.0, r1099333
Compiled: Wed May 4 07:57:50 PDT 2011 by oom
Identifier: 201108130335

Cluster Summary (Heap Size is 101.31 MB/888.94 MB)

Running Map Tasks	Running Reduce Tasks	Total Submissions	Nodes	Occupied Map Slots	Occupied Reduce Slots	Reserved Map Slots	Reserved Reduce Slots	Map Task Capacity	Reduce Task Capacity	Avg. Tasks/Node	Blacklisted Nodes	Graylisted Nodes	Excluded Nodes
0	0	2	1	0	0	0	0	2	2	4.00	0	0	0

Scheduling Information

Queue Name	State	Scheduling Information
default	running	N/A

Filter (Jobid, Priority, User, Name)
Example: 'user smith 3200' will filter by 'smith' only in the user field and '3200' in all fields

Running Jobs

Retired Jobs

Jobid	Priority	User	Name	State	Start Time	Finish Time	Map % Complete	Reduce % Complete	Job Scheduling Information	Diagnostic Info
job_201108130335_0002	NORMAL	hduser	streamjob367193073415596138.jar	SUCCEEDED	Sat Aug 13 03:50:48 UTC 2011	Sat Aug 13 03:57:07 UTC 2011	100.00%	100.00%	NA	NA
job_201108130335_0001	NORMAL	hduser	streamjob3850080991539619059.jar	FAILED	Sat Aug 13 03:36:56 UTC 2011	Sat Aug 13 03:40:17 UTC 2011	100.00%	100.00%	NA	NA

- Running Hadoop on Ubuntu Linux (*http://www.michael-noll.com/tutorials/running-hadoop-on-ubuntu-linux-single-node-cluster/*)

Hive (*http://hive.apache.org*)

With Hive, you can program Hadoop jobs using SQL. It's a great interface for anyone coming from the relational database world, though the details of the underlying implementation aren't completely hidden. You do still have to worry about some differences in things like the most optimal way to specify joins for best performance and some missing language features. Hive does offer the ability to plug in custom code for situations that don't fit into SQL, as well as a lot of tools for handling input and output. To use it, you set up structured tables that describe your input and output, issue load commands to ingest your files, and then write your queries as you would in any other relational database. Do be aware, though, that because of Hadoop's focus on large-scale processing, the latency may mean that even simple jobs take minutes to complete, so it's not a substitute for a real-time transactional database.

Pig (*http://pig.apache.org*)

The Apache Pig project is a procedural data processing language designed for Hadoop. In contrast to Hive's approach of writing logic-driven queries, with Pig you specify a series of steps to perform on the data. It's closer to an everyday scripting language, but with a specialized set of functions that help with common data processing problems. It's easy to break text up into component ngrams, for example, and then count up how often each occurs. Other frequently used operations, such as filters and joins, are also supported. Pig is typically used when your problem (or your inclination) fits with a procedural approach, but you need to do typical data processing operations, rather than general purpose calculations. Pig has been described as "the duct tape of Big Data" (*http://blog.linkedin.com/2010/07/01/linkedin-apache-pig/*) for its usefulness there, and it is often combined with custom streaming code written in a scripting language for more general operations.

Cascading (*http://www.cascading.org*)

Most real-world Hadoop applications are built of a series of processing steps, and Cascading lets you define that sort of complex workflow as a program. You lay out the logical flow of the data pipeline you need, rather than building it explicitly out of MapReduce steps feeding into one another. To use it, you call a Java API, connecting objects that represent the operations you want to perform into a graph. The system takes that definition, does some checking and planning, and executes it on your Hadoop cluster. There are a lot of built-in objects for common operations like sorting, grouping, and joining, and you can write your own objects to run custom processing code.

Cascalog (*https://github.com/nathanmarz/cascalog*)

Cascalog is a functional data processing interface written in Clojure. Influenced by the old Datalog language and built on top of the Cascading framework, it lets you write your processing code at a high level of abstraction while the system takes care of assembling it into a Hadoop job. It makes it easy to switch between local execution on small amounts of data to test your code and production jobs on your real Hadoop cluster. Cascalog inherits the same approach of input and output taps and processing operations from Cascading, and the functional paradigm seems like a natural way of specifying data flows. It's a distant descendant of the original Clojure wrapper for Cascading, cascading-clojure (*https://github.com/getwoven/cascading-clojure*).

mrjob (*https://github.com/Yelp/mrjob*)

Mrjob is a framework that lets you write the code for your data processing, and then transparently run it either locally, on Elastic MapReduce, or on your own Hadoop cluster. Written in Python, it doesn't offer the same level of abstraction or built-in operations as the Java-based Cascading. The job specifications are defined as a series of map and reduce steps, each implemented as a Python function. It is great as a framework for executing jobs, even allowing you to attach a debugger to local runs to really understand what's happening in your code.

Caffeine

Even though no significant technical information has been published on it, I'm including Google's Caffeine project, as there's a lot of speculation that it's a replacement for the MapReduce paradigm. From reports and company comments, it appears that Google is using a new version of the Google File System that supports smaller files and distributed masters. It also sounds like the company has moved away from the batch processing approach to building its search index, instead using a dynamic database approach to make updating faster. There's no indication that Google's come up with a new algorithmic approach that's as widely applicable as MapReduce, though I am looking forward to hearing more about the new architecture.

S4 (*http://s4.io*)

Yahoo! initially created the S4 system to make decisions about choosing and positioning ads, but the company open sourced it after finding it useful for processing arbitrary streams of events. S4 lets you write code to handle unbounded streams of events, and runs it distributed across a cluster of machines, using the ZooKeeper framework to handle the housekeeping details. You write data sources and handlers in Java, and S4 handles broadcasting the data as events across the system, load-balancing the work across the available machines. It's focused on returning results fast, with low latency, for applications like building near real-time search engines on rapidly changing content. This sets it apart from Hadoop and the general MapReduce approach, which involves synchronization steps within the pipeline, and so some degree of latency. One thing to be aware of is that S4 uses UDP and generally offers no delivery guarantees for the data that's passing through the pipeline. It usually seems possible to adjust queue sizes to avoid data loss, but it does put the burden of tuning to reach the required level of reliability on the application developer.

MapR (*http://www.mapr.com*)

MapR is a commercial distribution of Hadoop aimed at enterprises. It includes its own file systems that are a replacement for HDFS, along with other tweaks to the framework, like distributed name nodes for improved reliability. The new file system aims to offer increased performance, as well as easier backups and compatibility with NFS to make it simpler to transfer data in and out. The programming model is still the standard

Hadoop one; the focus is on improving the infrastructure surrounding the core framework to make it more appealing to corporate customers.

Acunu (*http://www.acunu.com/*)

Like MapR, Acunu is a new low-level data storage layer that replaces the traditional file system, though its initial target is Cassandra rather than Hadoop. By writing a kernel-level key/value store called Castle (*http://www.acunu.com/blogs/tom-wilkie/castle-storage-engine-oscon/*), which has been open-sourced (*https://bitbucket.org/acunu/fs.hg/*), the creators are able to offer impressive speed boosts in many cases. The data structures behind the performance gains are also impressive (*http://arxiv.org/abs/1103.4282*). Acunu also offers some of the traditional benefits of a commercially supported distribution, such as automatic configuration and other administration tools.

Flume (*https://github.com/cloudera/flume*)

One very common use of Hadoop is taking web server or other logs from a large number of machines, and periodically processing them to pull out analytics information. The Flume project is designed to make the data gathering process easy and scalable, by running agents on the source machines that pass the data updates to collectors, which then aggregate them into large chunks that can be efficiently written as HDFS files. It's usually set up using a command-line tool that supports common operations, like tailing a file or listening on a network socket, and has tunable reliability guarantees that let you trade off performance and the potential for data loss.

Kafka (*http://incubator.apache.org/kafka/index.html*)

Kafka is a comparatively new project for sending large numbers of events from producers to consumers. Originally built to connect LinkedIn's website with its backend systems, it's somewhere between S4 and Flume in its functionality. Unlike S4, it's persistent and offers more safeguards for delivery than Yahoo!'s UDP-based system, but it tries to retain its distributed nature and low latency. It can be used in a very similar way to Flume, keeping its high throughput, but with a more flexible system for creating multiple clients and an underlying architecture that's more focused on parallelization. Kafka relies on ZooKeeper to keep track of its distributed processing.

Azkaban (*http://sna-projects.com/azkaban/*)

The trickiest part of building a working system using these new data tools is the integration. The individual services need to be tied together into sequences of operations that are triggered by your business logic, and building that plumbing is surprisingly time consuming. Azkaban is an open source project from LinkedIn that lets you define what you want to happen as a job flow, possibly made up of many dependent steps, and then handles a lot of the messy housekeeping details. It keeps track of the log outputs, spots errors and emails about errors as they happen, and provides a friendly web interface so you can see how your jobs are getting on. Jobs are created as text files, using a very minimal set of commands, with any complexity expected to reside in the Unix commands or Java programs that the step calls.

Oozie (*http://yahoo.github.com/oozie/*)

Oozie is a job control system that's similar to Azkaban, but exclusively focused on Hadoop. This isn't as big a difference as you might think, since most Azkaban uses I've run across have also been for Hadoop, but it does mean that Oozie's integration is a bit tighter, especially if you're using the Yahoo! distribution of both. Oozie also supports a more complex language for describing job flows, allowing you to make runtime decisions about exactly which steps to perform, all described in XML files. There's also an API that you can use to build your own extensions to the system's functionality. Compared to Azkaban, Oozie's interface is more powerful but also more complex, so which you choose should depend on how much you need Oozie's advanced features.

Greenplum (*http://www.greenplum.com*)

Though not strictly a NoSQL database, the Greenplum system offers an interesting way of combining a flexible query language with distributed performance. Built on top of the Postgres open source database, it adds in a distributed architecture to run on a cluster of multiple machines, while retaining the standard SQL interface. It automatically shards rows across machines, by default based on a hash of a table's primary key, and works to avoid data loss both by using RAID drive setups on individual servers and by replicating data across machines. It's normally deployed on clusters of machines with comparatively fast processors and large amounts of RAM, in contrast to the pattern of using commodity hardware that's more common in the web world.

CHAPTER 4

Storage

Large-scale data processing operations access data in a way that traditional file systems are not designed for. Data tends to be written and read in large batches, multiple megabytes at once. Efficiency is a higher priority than features like directories that help organize information in a user-friendly way. The massive size of the data also means that it needs to be stored across multiple machines in a distributed way. As a result, several specialized technologies have appeared that support those needs and trade off some of the features of general purpose file systems required by POSIX standards.

S3 (*http://aws.amazon.com/s3*)

Amazon's S3 service lets you store large chunks of data on an online service, with an interface that makes it easy to retrieve the data over the standard web protocol, HTTP. One way of looking at it is as a file system that's missing some features like appending, rewriting or renaming files, and true directory trees. You can also see it as a key/value database available as a web service and optimized for storing large amounts of data in each value.

To give a concrete example, you could store the data for a *.png* image into the system using the API provided by Amazon. You'd first have to create a *bucket*, which is a bit like a global top-level directory that's owned by one user, and which must have a unique name. You'd then supply the bucket name, a file name (which can contain slashes, and so may appear like a file in a subdirectory), the data itself, and any metadata to create the object.

If you specified that the object was publicly accessible, you'd then be able to access it through any web browser at an address like *http://yourbucket.s3.amazonaws.com/your/file/name.png*. If you supplied the right content-type in the metadata, it would be displayed as an image to your browser.

I use S3 a lot because it's cheap, well-documented, reliable, fast, copes with large amounts of traffic, and is very easy to access from almost any environment, thanks to its support of HTTP for reads. In some applications I've even used it as a crude database, when I didn't need the ability to run queries and was only storing a comparatively small number of large data objects. It also benefits from Amazon's investment in user interfaces and APIs that have encouraged the growth of an ecosystem of tools.

- s3cmd: a command-line client for S3 (*http://s3tools.org/s3cmd*)
- s3sync: the equivalent of rsync for S3 (*http://s3sync.net/wiki*)

Hadoop Distributed File System (*http://hadoop.apache.org/hdfs*)

The Hadoop Distributed File System (HDFS) is designed to support applications like MapReduce jobs that read and write large amounts of data in batches, rather than more randomly accessing lots of small files. It abandons some POSIX requirements to achieve this, but unlike S3, it does support renaming and moving files, along with true directories. You can only write to a file once at creation time, to make it easier to handle coherency problems when the data's hosted on a cluster of machines, so that cached copies of the file can be read from any of the machines that have one, without having to check if the contents have changed. The client software stores up written data in a temporary local file, until there's enough to fill a complete HDFS *block*. All files are stored in these blocks, with a default size of 64 MB. Once enough data has been buffered, or the write operation is closed, the local data is sent across the network and written to multiple servers in the cluster, to ensure it isn't lost if there's a hardware failure.

To simplify the architecture, HDFS uses a single name node to keep track of which files are stored where. This does mean there's a single point of failure and potential performance bottleneck. In typical data processing applications, the metadata it's responsible for is small and not accessed often, so in practice this doesn't usually cause performance problems. The manual intervention needed for a name node failure can be a headache for system maintainers, though.

CHAPTER 5

Servers

"The cloud" is a very vague term, but there's been a real change in the availability of computing resources. Rather than the purchase or long-term leasing of a physical machine that used to be the norm, now it's much more common to rent computers that are being run as virtual instances. This makes it economical for the provider to offer very short-term rentals of flexible numbers of machines, which is ideal for a lot of data processing applications. Being able to quickly fire up a large cluster makes it possible to deal with very big data problems on a small budget. Since there are many companies with different approaches to this sort of server rental, I'll look at what they offer from the perspective of a data processing developer.

EC2 (*http://aws.amazon.com/ec2*)

In simple terms, EC2 lets you rent computers by the hour, with a choice of different memory and CPU configurations. You get network access to a complete Linux or Windows server that you can log into as root, allowing you to install software and flexibly configure the system. Under the hood these machines are actually hosted virtually, with many running on each physical server in the data center, which keeps the prices low. There are many other companies offering virtualized servers, but Amazon's EC2 stands out for data processing applications because of the ecosystem that's grown up around it. It has a rich set of third-party virtual machine snapshots to start with and easy integration with S3, both through a raw interface and through the Elastic Block Storage (EBS) wrapper, which uses S3 to back something that looks like a traditional filesystem. The Elastic MapReduce service makes it easy to create temporary Hadoop clusters. You can even upload very large data sets from physical media that you post to Amazon!

The biggest drawback to hosting your computation on the service is that you have little control over the true hardware layout of any clusters you create, thanks to the virtualization layer. I often find that my Hadoop jobs are bottlenecked by network communication and data transfer, and so it makes more sense to use a larger number of lower-spec machines, rather than the somewhat more capable servers you'd probably choose for an in-house Hadoop cluster. Amazon's spot instance (*http://aws.amazon.com/ec2/*

spot-instances/) auction pricing model is a great fit for background data processing jobs. You can often get servers at a third of the normal cost, and the loss of machines if demand picks up is an inconvenience, not a disaster.

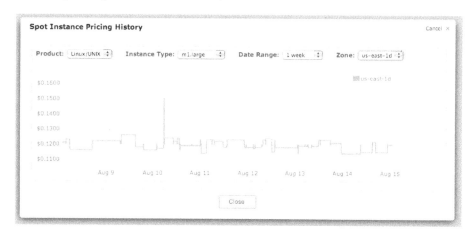

- EC2 for poets (*http://scripting.com/opmlHowto/dave/ec2/*)

Google App Engine (*http://code.google.com/appengine*)

With Google's App Engine service, you write your web-serving code in either Java, a JVM language, or Python, and it takes care of running the application in a scalable way so that it can cope with large numbers of simultaneous requests. Unlike with EC2 or traditional web hosting, you have very limited control over the environment your code is running in. This makes it easy to distribute across a lot of machines to handle heavy loads, since only your code needs to be transferred, but it does make it tough to run anything that needs flexible access to the underlying system. With traditional hosting, all your code is running on a single machine, and so you are naturally restricted to the storage and CPU time available on that machine. Since App Engine can run your code across a potentially unrestricted number of machines, Google has had to introduce a fairly complex system of quotas and billing to control applications' use of those resources. Since the system was originally designed to host web services handling a large number of short-lived page requests, some of these quota limits can be tough for data processing applications. For a long time, no request could run for more than 30 seconds, and though this has now been lifted for background requests, other restrictions still make it tough to run data processing or transfer-intensive code.

- Getting started with App Engine (*http://code.google.com/appengine/docs/python/gettingstarted/*)

Elastic Beanstalk (*http://aws.amazon.com/elasticbeanstalk*)

Elastic Beanstalk is a layer on top of the EC2 service that takes care of setting up an automatically scaling cluster of web servers behind a load balancer, allowing developers to deploy Java-based applications without worrying about a lot of the housekeeping details. This high-level approach makes it similar to App Engine and Heroku, but because it's just a wrapper for EC2, you can also log directly into the machines that the code is running on, to debug problems or tweak the environment. It's still fundamentally designed around the needs of frontend web applications, though, so most data processing problems aren't a good fit for its approach.

- Getting started with Elastic Beanstalk (*http://blog.teamextension.com/getting-star ted-with-aws-elastic-beanstalk-179*)

Heroku (*http://www.heroku.com*)

Heroku hosts Ruby web applications, offering a simple deployment process, a lot of free and paid plug-ins, and easy scalability. To ensure that your code can be quickly deployed across a large number of machines, there are some restrictions on things like access to the underlying filesystem, but in general the environment is more flexible than App Engine. You can install almost any Ruby gem, even those with native code, and you get a real SQL database rather than Google's scalable but restrictive alternative datastore. Heroku is still focused on the needs of frontend applications, though, so it's likely to be restricted to providing the interface to a data processing application. In particular, you may well hit its hard 300 MB memory limit if you start to perform operations that are too RAM intensive.

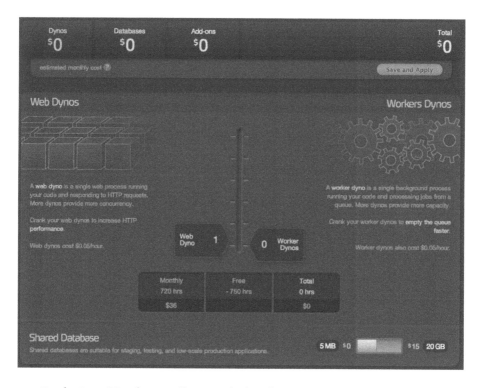

- Deploying a Heroku app (*http://web.elctech.com/?p=413*)

CHAPTER 6

Processing

Getting the concise, valuable information you want from a sea of data can be challenging, but there's been a lot of progress around systems that help you turn your datasets into something that makes sense. Because there are so many different barriers, the tools range from rapid statistical analysis systems to enlisting human helpers.

R (*http://www.r-project.org*)

The R project is both a specialized language and a toolkit of modules aimed at anyone working with statistics. It covers everything from loading your data to running sophisticated analyses on it and then either exporting or visualizing the results. The interactive shell makes it easy to experiment with your data, since you can try out a lot of different approaches very quickly. The biggest downside from a data processing perspective is that it's designed to work with datasets that fit within a single machine's memory. It is possible to use it within Hadoop as another streaming language, but a lot of the most powerful features require access to the complete dataset to be effective. R makes a great prototyping platform for designing solutions that need to run on massive amounts of data, though, or for making sense of the smaller-scale results of your processing.

Yahoo! Pipes (*http://pipes.yahoo.com/pipes*)

It's been several years since Yahoo! released the Pipes environment, but it's still an unsurpassed tool for building simple data pipelines. It has a graphical interface where you drag and drop components, linking them together into flows of processing operations. A lot of Yahoo!'s interesting APIs are exposed as building blocks, as well as components for importing web pages and RSS feeds and outputting the results as dynamic feeds. As a free tool aimed at technically minded consumers, Pipes can't handle massive datasets, but it's the equivalent of duct tape for a lot of smaller tasks. Similar but more specialized tools like Alpine Miner (*http://alpineminer.org/*) have had a lot of success in the commercial world, so I'm hopeful that the Pipes style of interface will show up more often in data processing applications.

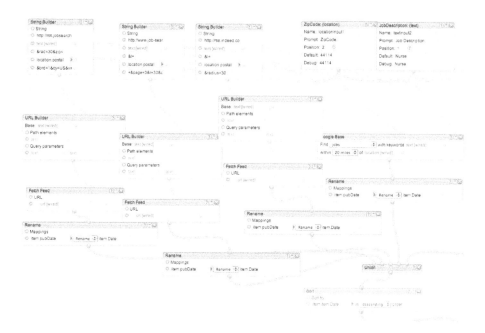

- Using YQL and Yahoo! Pipes together (*http://developer.yahoo.com/blogs/ydn/posts/2011/01/quick-tutorial-yql-pipes-working-together/*)

Mechanical Turk (*https://www.mturk.com/mturk/welcome*)

The original Mechanical Turk was a fraudulent device that appeared to be a chess-playing robot but was actually controlled by a hidden midget. Amazon's service exploits the same principle, recognizing that there are some mental tasks that it's most effective to ask real humans to perform. It can cost as little as a few cents per operation, depending on the duration and complexity of each small job you want performed. The low cost can make it feel a bit exploitative of the workers, but it's an incredibly powerful way of introducing genuine intelligence into your pipeline. Often you'll have a crucial problem that's not yet reliably solvable with AI but can be quickly done by a person. For example, you could feed in photos to get estimates of gender and age, something that you just can't do reliably using pure code. You do have to put in more thought and planning before you integrate it into your pipeline, since even at comparatively cheap rates it's a lot more expensive per operation. It can't be beaten as a get-out-of-jail-free card for when you encounter stubbornly AI-complete problems, though.

- RTurk: a Ruby library for Mechanical Turk tasks (*https://github.com/mdp/rturk*)

Solr/Lucene (*http://lucene.apache.org/solr*)

Lucene is a Java library that handles indexing and searching large collections of documents, and Solr is an application that uses the library to build a search engine server. Originally separate projects, they were recently merged into a single Apache open source team. It's designed to handle very big amounts of data, with a sharding architecture that means it will scale horizontally across a cluster of machines. It also has a very flexible plug-in architecture and configuration system, and it can be integrated with a lot of different data sources. These features, along with a well-tested code base, make it a great choice for anyone who needs to solve a large-scale search problem.

ElasticSearch (*http://www.elasticsearch.org*)

Like Solr, ElasticSearch is a search engine service that's built on top of Lucene. It's a younger project, aimed more at people in the web world (in contrast to Solr's heavy use in enterprises). It allows you to update the search index with much lower latency, has a more minimal REST/JSON-based interface and configuration options, and scales horizontally in a more seamless way. It doesn't yet have the community or number of contributors of the more established project, though, and it is missing some of the broader features that Solr offers, so it's worth evaluating both.

Datameer (*http://www.datameer.com*)

Though it's aimed at the well-known business intelligence market, Datameer is interesting because it uses Hadoop to power its processing. It offers a simplified programming environment for its operators to specify the kind of analysis they want, and then handles converting that into MapReduce jobs behind the scenes. It also has some user-friendly data importing tools, as well as visualization options. It's a sign of where data processing solutions are headed, as we get better at building interfaces and moving to higher and more powerful abstraction levels.

BigSheets (*http://www-01.ibm.com/software/ebusiness/ jstart/bigsheets/index.html*)

IBM's BigSheets is a web application that lets nontechnical users gather unstructured data from online and internal sources and analyze it to create reports and visualizations. Like Datameer, it uses Hadoop behind the scenes to handle very large amounts of data, along with services like OpenCalais to cope with extracting useful structured information from a soup of unstructured text. It's aimed at users who are comfortable with a spreadsheet interface rather than traditional developers, so it's not possible to use it as part of a custom solution, but does offer ideas on how to make your data processing application accessible to those sort of ordinary users.

Tinkerpop (*http://tinkerpop.com/*)

A group of developers working on open source graph software, Tinkerpop has produced an integrated suite of tools. A bit like the LAMP stack for graph processing, they're designing a set of services that work well together to perform common operations like interfacing to specialized graph databases, writing traversal queries, and exposing the whole system as a REST-based server. If you're dealing with graph data, Tinkerpop will give you some high-level interfaces that can be much more convenient to deal with than raw graph databases.

CHAPTER 7

NLP

Natural language processing (NLP) is a subset of data processing that's so crucial, it earned its own section. Its focus is taking messy, human-created text and extracting meaningful information. As you can imagine, this chaotic problem domain has spawned a large variety of approaches, with each tool most useful for particular kinds of text. There's no magic bullet that will understand written information as well as a human, but if you're prepared to adapt your use of the results to handle some errors and don't expect miracles, you can pull out some powerful insights.

Natural Language Toolkit (*http://www.nltk.org*)

The NLTK is a collection of Python modules and datasets that implement common natural language processing techniques. It offers the building blocks that you need to build more complex algorithms for specific problems. For example, you can use it to break up texts into sentences, break sentences into words, stem words by removing common suffixes (like *-ing* from English verbs), or use machine-readable dictionaries to spot synonyms. The framework is used by most researchers in the field, so you'll often find cutting-edge approaches included as modules or as algorithms built from its modules. There are also a large number of compatible datasets (*http://nltk.googlecode .com/svn/trunk/nltk_data/index.xml*) available, as well as ample documentation (*http:// www.nltk.org/documentation*).

NLTK isn't aimed at developers looking for an off-the-shelf solution to domain-specific problems. Its flexibility does mean you need a basic familiarity with the NLP world before you can create solutions for your own problems. It's not a prepackaged solution like Boilerpipe or OpenCalais.

OpenNLP (*http://incubator.apache.org/opennlp*)

Written in Java, OpenNLP is an alternative to NLTK for language processing. It has a stronger focus on prebuilt solutions, with models available (*http://opennlp.sourceforge*

.net/models-1.5/) that make it easy to do tasks like extracting times, people, and organization names from text. This approach does make it less appealing as a teaching framework, but the ease of integration with Java means it's a lot more suitable for applications written in the language. It does contain all of the standard components you need to build your own language-processing code, breaking the raw text down into sentences and words, and classifying those components using a variety of techniques.

Boilerpipe (*http://code.google.com/p/boilerpipe*)

One of the hardest parts of analyzing web pages is removing the navigation links, headers, footers, and sidebars to leave the meaningful content text. If all of that boilerplate is left in, the analysis will be highly distorted by repeated irrelevant words and phrases from those sections. Boilerpipe is a Java framework that uses an algorithmic approach to spotting the actual content of an HTML document, and so makes a great preprocessing tool for any web content. It's aimed at pages that look something like a news story, but I've found it works decently for many different types of sites.

- A live demonstration of the service (*http://boilerpipe-web.appspot.com/*)

OpenCalais (*http://www.opencalais.com/*)

OpenCalais is a web API that takes a piece of text, spots the names of entities it knows about, and suggests overall tags. It's a mature project run by Thomson Reuters and is widely used. In my experience, it tends to be strongest at understanding terms and phrases that you might see in formal news stories, as you might expect from its heritage. It's definitely a good place to start when you need a semantic analysis of your content, but there are still some reasons you might want to look into alternatives. There is a 50,000 per-day limit on calls, and 100K limit on document sizes for the standard API. This is negotiable with the commercial version, but the overhead is one reason to consider running something on a local cluster instead for large volumes of data. You may also need to ensure that the content you're submitting is not sensitive, though the service does promise not to retain any of it (*http://www.opencalais.com/privacy*). There may also be a set of terms or phrases unique to your problem domain that's not covered by the service. In that case, a hand-rolled parser built on NLTK or OpenNLP could be a better solution.

CHAPTER 8

Machine Learning

Another important processing category, machine learning systems automate decision making on data. They use training information to deal with subsequent data points, automatically producing outputs like recommendations or groupings. These systems are especially useful when you want to turn the results of a one-off data analysis into a production service that will perform something similar on new data without supervision. Some of the most famous uses of these techniques are features like Amazon's product recommendations.

WEKA (*http://www.cs.waikato.ac.nz/ml/weka*)

WEKA is a Java-based framework and GUI for machine learning algorithms. It provides a plug-in architecture for researchers to add their own techniques, with a command-line and window interface that makes it easy to apply them to your own data. You can use it to do everything from basic clustering to advanced classification, together with a lot of tools for visualizing your results. It is heavily used as a teaching tool, but it also comes in extremely handy for prototyping and experimenting outside of the classroom. It has a strong set of preprocessing tools that make it easy to load your data in, and then you have a large library of algorithms at your fingertips, so you can quickly try out ideas until you find an approach that works for your problem. The command-line interface allows you to apply exactly the same code in an automated way for production.

Mahout (*http://mahout.apache.org*)

Mahout is an open source framework that can run common machine learning algorithms on massive datasets. To achieve that scalability, most of the code is written as parallelizable jobs on top of Hadoop. It comes with algorithms to perform a lot of common tasks, like clustering and classifying objects into groups, recommending items based on other users' behaviors, and spotting attributes that occur together a lot. In practical terms, the framework makes it easy to use analysis techniques to implement features such as Amazon's "People who bought this also bought" recommendation engine on your own site. It's a heavily used project with an active community of developers and users, and it's well worth trying if you have any significant number of transaction or similar data that you'd like to get more value out of.

- Introducing Mahout (*http://www.ibm.com/developerworks/java/library/j-mahout/*)
- Using Mahout with Cassandra (*http://www.acunu.com/blogs/sean-owen/recom mending-cassandra/*)

scikits.learn (*http://scikit-learn.sourceforge.net/stable/*)

It's hard to find good off-the-shelf tools for practical machine learning. Many of the projects are aimed at students and researchers who want access to the inner workings of the algorithms, which can be off-putting when you're looking for more of a black box to solve a particular problem. That's a gap that scikits.learn really helps to fill. It's a beautifully documented (*http://scikit-learn.sourceforge.net/stable/tutorial.html*) and easy-to-use Python package offering a high-level interface to many standard machine learning techniques. It collects most techniques that fall under the standard definition of machine learning (taking a training dataset and using that to predict something useful about data received later) and offers a common way of connecting them together and swapping them out. This makes it a very fruitful sandbox for experimentation and rapid prototyping, with a very easy path to using the same code in production once it's working well.

- Face Recognition using scikits.learn (*http://scikit-learn.sourceforge.net/stable/auto _examples/applications/face_recognition.html*)

CHAPTER 9

Visualization

One of the best ways to communicate the meaning of data is by extracting the important parts and presenting them graphically. This is helpful both for internal use, as an exploration technique to spot patterns that aren't obvious from the raw values, and as a way to succinctly present end users with understandable results. As the Web has turned graphs from static images to interactive objects, the lines between presentation and exploration have blurred. The possibilities of the new medium have led to some of the fantastic new tools I cover in this section.

Gephi (*http://gephi.org*)

Gephi is an open source Java application that creates network visualizations from raw edge and node graph data. It's very useful for understanding social network information; one of the project's founders was hired by LinkedIn, and Gephi is now used for LinkedIn visualizations. There are several different layout algorithms, each with multiple parameters you can tweak to arrange the positions of the nodes in your data. If there are any manual changes you want to make, to either the input data or the positioning, you can do that through the data laboratory, and once you've got your basic graph laid out, the preview tab lets you customize the exact appearance of the rendered result. Though Gephi is best known for its window interface, you can also script a lot of its functions from automated backend tools, using its toolkit library (*http://gephi.org/toolkit/*).

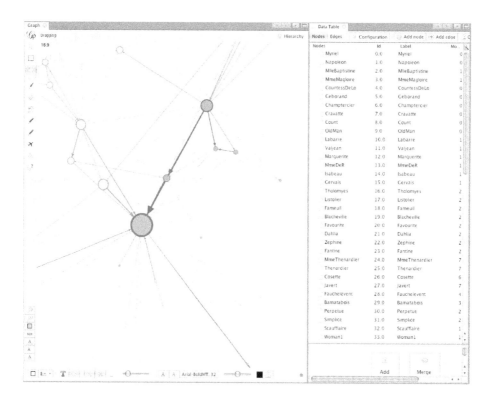

GraphViz (*http://www.graphviz.org*)

GraphViz is a command-line network graph visualization tool. It's mostly used for general purpose flowchart and tree diagrams rather than the less structured graphs that Gephi's known for. It also produces comparatively ugly results by default, though there are options to pretty-up the fonts, line rendering, and drop shadows. Despite those cosmetic drawbacks, GraphViz is still a very powerful tool for producing diagrams from data. Its DOT file specification has been adopted as an interchange format by a lot of programs, making it easy to plug into many tools, and it has sophisticated algorithms for laying out even massive numbers of nodes.

Processing (*http://processing.org*)

Initially best known as a graphics programming language that was accessible to designers, Processing has become a popular general-purpose tool for creating interactive web visualizations. It has accumulated a rich ecosystem of libraries, examples, and documentation, so you may well be able to find an existing template for the kind of information display you need for your data.

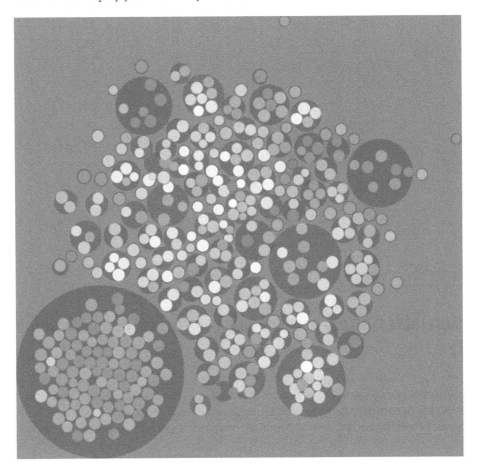

Protovis (*http://vis.stanford.edu/protovis*)

Protovis is a JavaScript framework packed full of ready-to-use visualization components like bar and line graphs, force-directed layouts of networks, and other common building blocks. It's great as a high-level interface to a toolkit of existing visualization templates, but compared to Processing, it's not as easy to build completely new components. Its developers have recently announced that Protovis will no longer be under active development, as they focus their efforts on the D3 library (*http://mbostock.github .com/d3/*), which offers similar functionality but in a style heavily influenced by the new generation of JavaScript frameworks like jQuery.

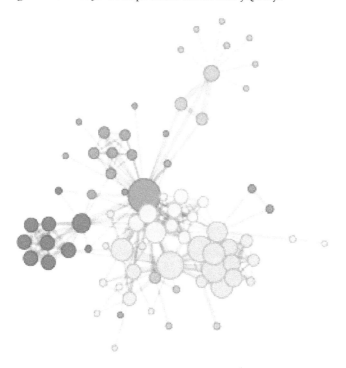

Fusion Tables (*http://www.google.com/fusiontables/Home?pli =1*)

Google has created an integrated online system that lets you store large amounts of data in spreadsheet-like tables and gives you tools to process and visualize the information. It's particularly good at turning geographic data into compelling maps, with the ability to upload your own custom KML outlines for areas like political constituencies. There is also a full set of traditional graphing tools, as well as a wide variety of options to perform calculations on your data. Fusion Tables is a powerful system, but it's definitely aimed at fairly technical users; the sheer variety of controls can be intimidating at first. If you're looking for a flexible tool to make sense of large amounts of data, it's worth making the effort.

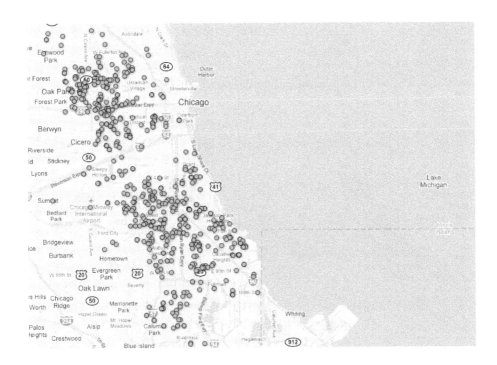

Tableau (*http://www.tableausoftware.com*)

Originally a traditional desktop application for drawing graphs and visualizations, Tableau has been adding a lot of support for online publishing and content creation. Its embedded graphs have become very popular with news organizations on the Web, illustrating a lot of stories. The support for geographic data isn't as extensive as Fusion's, but Tableau is capable of creating some map styles that Google's product can't produce. If you want the power user features of a desktop interface or are focused on creating graphics for professional publication, Tableau is a good choice.

Tableau | 39

Tale of 100 Entrepreneurs

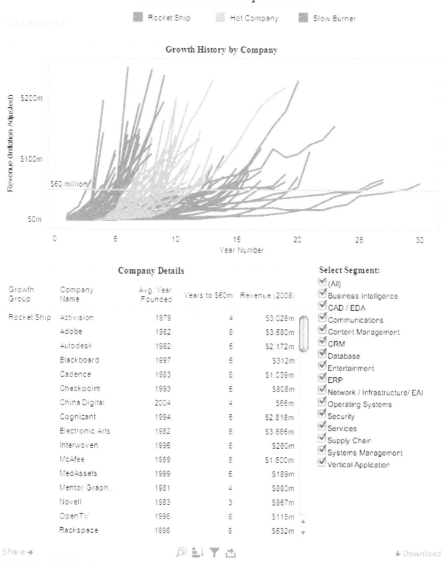

Rocket Ship   Hot Company   Slow Burner

Growth History by Company

Company Details

Growth Group	Company Name	Avg. Year Founded	Years to $50m	Revenue (2008)
Rocket Ship	Activision	1979	4	$3,026m
	Adobe	1982	6	$3,580m
	Autodesk	1982	5	$2,172m
	Blackboard	1997	5	$312m
	Cadence	1983	6	$1,039m
	Checkpoint	1993	5	$808m
	China Digital	2004	4	$55m
	Cognizant	1994	5	$2,816m
	Electronic Arts	1982	6	$3,665m
	Interwoven	1995	6	$260m
	McAfee	1989	6	$1,600m
	MedAssets	1999	5	$189m
	Mentor Graph..	1981	4	$880m
	Novell	1983	3	$957m
	OpenTV	1996	6	$116m
	Rackspace	1998	6	$532m

Select Segment:

- ☑ (All)
- ☑ Business Intelligence
- ☑ CAD / EDA
- ☑ Communications
- ☑ Content Management
- ☑ CRM
- ☑ Database
- ☑ Entertainment
- ☑ ERP
- ☑ Network / Infrastructure/ EAI
- ☑ Operating Systems
- ☑ Security
- ☑ Services
- ☑ Supply Chain
- ☑ Systems Management
- ☑ Vertical Application

Share →

↓ Download

⁺₊⁺ tableau

CHAPTER 10

Acquisition

Most of the interesting public data sources are poorly structured, full of noise, and hard to access. I probably spend more time turning messy source data into something usable than I do on the rest of the data analysis processes combined, so I'm very thankful that there are multiple tools emerging to help.

Google Refine (*http://code.google.com/p/google-refine*)

Google Refine is an update to the Freebase Gridworks tool for cleaning up large, messy spreadsheets. It has been designed to make it easy to correct the most common errors you'll encounter in human-created datasets. For example, it's easy to spot and correct common problems like typos or inconsistencies in text values and to change cells from one format to another. There's also rich support for linking data by calling APIs with the data contained in existing rows to augment the spreadsheet with information from external sources.

Refine doesn't let you do anything you can't with other tools, but its power comes from how well it supports a typical extract and transform workflow. It feels like a good step up in abstraction, packaging processes that would typically take multiple steps in a scripting language or spreadsheet package into single operations with sensible defaults.

Needlebase (*http://www.needlebase.com*)

Needlebase provides a point-and-click interface for extracting structured information from web pages. As a user, you select elements on an example page that contain the data you're interested in, and the tool then uses the patterns you've defined to pull out information from other pages on a site with a similar structure. For example, you might want to extract product names and prices from a shopping site. With the tool, you could find a single product page, select the product name and price, and then the same elements would be pulled for every other page it crawled from the site. It relies on the fact that most web pages are generated by combining templates with information retrieved from a database, and so have a very consistent structure.

Once you've gathered the data, it offers some features that are a bit like Google Refine's for de-duplicating and cleaning up the data. All in all, it's a very powerful tool for turning web content into structured information, with a very approachable interface.

ScraperWiki (*http://scraperwiki.com*)

ScraperWiki is a hosted environment for writing automated processes to scan public websites and extract structured information from the pages they've published. It handles all of the boilerplate code that you normally have to write to handle crawling websites, gives you a simple online editor for your Ruby, Python, or PHP scripts, and automatically runs your crawler as a background process. What I really like, though, is the way that most of the scripts are published on the site, so new users have a lot of existing examples to start with, and as websites change their structures, popular older scrapers can be updated by the community.

CHAPTER 11

Serialization

As you work on turning your data into something useful, it will have to pass between various systems and probably be stored in files at various points. These operations all require some kind of serialization, especially since different stages of your processing are likely to require different languages and APIs. When you're dealing with very large numbers of records, the choices you make about how to represent and store them can have a massive impact on your storage requirements and performance.

JSON (*http://www.json.org*)

Though it's well known to most web developers, JSON (JavaScript Object Notation) has only recently emerged as a popular format for data processing. Its biggest advantages are that it maps trivially to existing data structures in most languages and it has a layout that's restrictive enough to keep the parsing code and schema design simple, but with enough flexibility to express most data in a fairly natural way. Its simplicity does come with some costs, though, especially in storage size. If you're representing a list of objects mapping keys to values, the most intuitive way would be to use an indexed array of associative arrays. This means that the string for each key is stored inside each object, which involves a large number of duplicated strings when the number of unique keys is small compared to the number of values. There are manual ways around this, of course, especially as the textual representations usually compress well, but many of the other serialization approaches I'll talk about try to combine the flexibility of JSON with a storage mechanism that's more space efficient.

BSON (*http://www.bsonspec.org*)

Originally created by the team behind MongoDB, and still used in its storage engine, the BSON (Binary JSON) specification can represent any JSON object in a binary form. Interestingly, the main design goal was not space efficiency, but speed of conversion. A lot of parsing time can be saved during loading and saving by storing integers and doubles in their native binary representations rather than as text strings. There's also native support for types that have no equivalent in JSON, like blobs of raw binary information and dates.

Thrift (*http://incubator.apache.org/thrift*)

With Thrift, you predefine both the structure of your data objects and the interfaces you'll be using to interact with them. The system then generates code to serialize and deserialize the data and stub functions that implement the entry points to your interfaces. It generates efficient code for a wide variety of languages, and under the hood offers a lot of choices for the underlying data format without affecting the application layer. It has proven to be a popular IDL (Interface Definition Language) for open source infrastructure projects like Cassandra and HDFS. It can feel a bit overwhelming for smaller teams working on lightweight projects, though. Much like statically-typed languages, using a predefined IDL requires investing some time up front in return for strong documentation, future bug prevention, and performance gains. That makes the choice very dependent on the expected lifetime and number of developers on your project.

Avro (*http://avro.apache.org*)

A newer competitor to Thrift, and also under the Apache umbrella, Avro offers similar functionality but with very different design tradeoffs. You still define a schema for your data and the interfaces you'll use, but instead of being held separately within each program, the schema is transmitted alongside the data. That makes it possible to write code that can handle arbitrary data structures, rather than only the types that were known when the program was created. This flexibility does come at the cost of space and performance efficiency when encoding and decoding the information. Avro schemas are defined using JSON, which can feel a bit clunky compared to more domain-specific IDLs, though there is experimental support for a more user-friendly format known as Avro IDL (*http://avro.apache.org/docs/1.4.0/idl.html*).

Protocol Buffers (*http://code.google.com/p/protobuf*)

An open sourced version of the system that Google uses internally on most of its projects, the Protocol Buffers stack is an IDL similar to Thrift. One difference is that Thrift includes network client and server code in its generated stubs, whereas *protobuf* limits its scope to pure serialization and deserialization. The biggest differentiator between the two projects is probably their developer base. Though the code is open source, Google is the main contributor and driver for Protocol Buffers, whereas Thrift is more of a classic crowd-sourced project. If your requirements skew towards stability and strong documentation, Protocol Buffers is going to be attractive, whereas if you need a more open, community-based approach, Thrift will be a lot more appealing.

About the Author

A former Apple engineer, **Pete Warden** is the founder of OpenHeatMap, and he writes on large-scale data processing and visualization.

Get even more for your money.

Join the O'Reilly Community, and register the O'Reilly books you own. It's free, and you'll get:

- $4.99 ebook upgrade offer
- 40% upgrade offer on O'Reilly print books
- Membership discounts on books and events
- Free lifetime updates to ebooks and videos
- Multiple ebook formats, DRM FREE
- Participation in the O'Reilly community
- Newsletters
- Account management
- 100% Satisfaction Guarantee

Signing up is easy:

1. Go to: oreilly.com/go/register
2. Create an O'Reilly login.
3. Provide your address.
4. Register your books.

Note: English-language books only

To order books online:
oreilly.com/store

For questions about products or an order:
orders@oreilly.com

To sign up to get topic-specific email announcements and/or news about upcoming books, conferences, special offers, and new technologies:
elists@oreilly.com

For technical questions about book content:
booktech@oreilly.com

To submit new book proposals to our editors:
proposals@oreilly.com

O'Reilly books are available in multiple DRM-free ebook formats. For more information:
oreilly.com/ebooks

Spreading the knowledge of innovators   oreilly.com

©2010 O'Reilly Media, Inc. O'Reilly logo is a registered trademark of O'Reilly Media, Inc. 00000

The information you need, when and where you need it.

With Safari Books Online, you can:

Access the contents of thousands of technology and business books

- Quickly search over 7000 books and certification guides
- Download whole books or chapters in PDF format, at no extra cost, to print or read on the go
- Copy and paste code
- Save up to 35% on O'Reilly print books
- **New!** Access mobile-friendly books directly from cell phones and mobile devices

Stay up-to-date on emerging topics before the books are published

- Get on-demand access to evolving manuscripts.
- Interact directly with authors of upcoming books

Explore thousands of hours of video on technology and design topics

- Learn from expert video tutorials
- Watch and replay recorded conference sessions

Spreading the knowledge of innovators   safari.oreilly.com

©2009 O'Reilly Media, Inc. O'Reilly logo is a registered trademark of O'Reilly Media, Inc. 00000

Ingram Content Group UK Ltd.
Milton Keynes UK
UKHW032253240423
420706UK00009B/145